THE *Living* Mass

Changes to the Roman Missal and How We Worship

FATHER HELIODORO LUCATERO

Liguori
ONE LIGUORI DRIVE
LIGUORI MO 63057-9999

Imprimi Potest: Harry Grile, CSsR
Provincial, Denver Province, The Redemptorists

Imprimatur: "In accordance with c. 827, permission to publish has been granted
on March 16, 2011, by the Most Reverend Robert J. Hermann, Auxiliary Bishop
Emeritus, Archdiocese of St. Louis. Permission to publish is an indication that
nothing contrary to Church teaching is contained in this work. It does not imply
any endorsement of the opinions expressed in the publication; nor is any liability
assumed by this permission."

Published by Liguori Publications
Liguori, Missouri 63057
To order, call 800-325-9521, or visit liguori.org.

Library of Congress Cataloging-in-Publication Data

Lucatero, Heliodoro.
   The living Mass : changes to the Roman missal and how we worship /
Heliodoro Lucatero.
      p. cm.
   ISBN 978-0-7648-2007-6
   1. Catholic Church. Missale Romanum (1970) 2. Catholic Church—Liturgy—
Texts—History and criticism. 3. Mass. I. Title.
   BX2015.L79 2011
   264'.023—dc22

                                                                    2011008416

Compliant with the *Roman Missal,* third edition.

Liguori Publications, a nonprofit corporation, is an apostolate of the
Redemptorists. To learn more about the Redemptorists, visit Redemptorists.com.

Printed in the United States of America
15 14 13 12 11   /   5 4 3 2
First edition

CONTENTS

Introduction   5

Brief History of the Mass and of the *Roman Missal*   8

The Apostolic Period   8

From the Fourth Century to the Middle Ages   12

Middle Ages to the Sixteenth Century   14

From the Council of Trent to the Second Vatican Council   17

The Second Vatican Council   20

The 1970 *Roman Missal of Paul VI*   21

The First Edition of the *Roman Missal* in 1974   24

The Second Edition of the *Roman Missal* in 1985   25

The 2002 Third Edition of the *Roman Missal*   26

**The New Translation Based on the Third Edition
of the *Roman Missal*   27**

Why a New Translation?   27

Who Makes the Translations?   28

What Changes Will the New Translation Have?   29

The Greeting   32

The Penitential Rite   34

The Gloria   36

The Gospel's Response   38

The Nicene-Constantinopolitan Creed   40

The Apostles' Creed   44

The *Suscipiat Dominus* (May the Lord accept the sacrifice
    at your hands...)   46
The Dialogue of the Preface   48
The *Sanctus* (Holy, holy, holy...)   50
The Mystery of Faith (The Memorial Acclamation)   52
The *Agnus Dei* (This is the Lamb of God...)   54

What Are Some of the Criteria
That Will be Used for the Liturgical Translations?   57

Comme le Prévoit, 1969   57
Liturgiam Authenticam, 2001   59
Ratio Translationis, 2007   60

Conclusion   63

INTRODUCTION

From the moment we heard rumors there would be changes to the *Roman Missal*, the book the priest uses for the different prayers of the Mass, people started to ask the reasons for the changes and what changes would be introduced to the way that the celebration of the Eucharist was presented.

First, it would be good to make clear an important point. The rite of the Mass will not change. We should also mention that the rite of the Mass that has been celebrated has seen changes throughout the centuries. For instance, the manner in which the Lord's Supper was celebrated in the first years after Christ's resurrection has been evolving for centuries.

The last significant changes to the Mass took place toward the end of the 1960s and were dictated by the liturgical reform of the Second Vatican Council. Also, it is good to clarify that even though the Mass has had many changes, the vital parts of the Mass have not changed, nor will they change. What is vital? The Word of God and the Eucharist or the Lord's Supper.

Thus the changes we will speak about in this book deal with linguistics, meaning that there are only some changes to the present form of how we say the prayers and how the assembly responds to the dialogs that are between them and the priest. Some formats that are prayed during the Mass are the Glory Be and the Creed.

It is important to note that the new version in Spanish will not have as many changes as will the new *Missal* in English. Since the Spanish language is derived from the Latin, a romance language, it is more similar to the Latin than the English; thus the new English translation will have more changes.

Toward the end of the 1980s, there were some adaptations to the Spanish *Missal*, specifically the Ordinary of the Mass; this was called the "unique text." This text was a translation of the Ordinary of the Mass, which was made equally for all Spanish-speaking countries. While parts of the Mass in Spanish will not change much, the prayers that the priest says in the Mass will be from the new translation.

As far as what changes are being made and why they are being made to the *Roman Missal*, which the Church calls the third edition, this book has as its objective the presentation of a brief history of the Mass throughout the centuries, from the beginning of the celebration of the Mass by the first disciples of Jesus through the fulfillment of his command: "Do this in memory of me," and continuing through the first centuries of the early Church, the Patristic Era, the Middle Ages, the Renaissance, with its turbulent moments due to the Protestant Reformation, and the Counter-Reformation of the Catholic Church. This reform took the Church to an Ecumenical Council, the Council of Trent, that reformed the liturgy, and the result of this reform was the *Roman Missal* that would be used from the sixteenth through the twentieth centuries.

There also was reform in the Second Vatican Council that not only introduced several changes to the liturgy but also a new book called the *Paul VI Missal*.

The objective of this historical review is to verify that during the history of the Church changes have been brought about that are not arbitrary but that form part of the natural evolution of a living entity: the liturgy. The changes that came about through the years have been very well thought of and have responded to the different needs of the Christian community in the different moments of history.

Another objective of this book is to show why the people of God seek new forms of verbal expressions to communicate the liturgy. We shall also see the criterion and the norms that are used for a new translation: who makes the translations; who approves them and why. Hopefully, at the end of our study, we shall have a better idea that the liturgy is a living entity. The liturgy must constantly grow and evolve in order to adapt to the reality of those who answer God's call, which sanctifies us, to praise him and bless him while we, as pilgrims in this world, wait for our Lord Jesus Christ at the end of time. The improvements that have been given through the centuries illustrate that our liturgy is alive. We will also discover that the changes in translation in this third edition are relatively small in comparison to the changes of the past. Finally, we shall see several examples of these changes in the language of the new translation of the third edition of the *Roman Missal*.

Now let us begin our journey through the history of the *Roman Missal* in the Catholic Church through the centuries, beginning with the Apostolic Period.

BRIEF HISTORY OF THE MASS AND OF THE *ROMAN MISSAL*

The Apostolic Period

Upon initiating this brief historic review of the evolution of the Mass, one must clarify that since the beginning, not only were there changes made through the years, but also a great variety of rites or formats of celebrating the Mass were developed. This is a reality that still exists in today's Christianity. We may think that the only format of celebrating Mass is the one we know, which comes from the Roman rite. However, that is not so. There are many other rites and formats of celebrating the Mass in the Catholic Church, including the Mozarabic rite in Spain, the Ambrosian rite in Milan, the Coptic rite in Egypt, the Byzantine rite in Greece, the Maronite rite in Lebanon, the Syro-Malabar rite in the Southeast of India, and many more. In our review, we shall limit ourselves to the evolution of the Mass in the Roman rite.

After Jesus' Last Supper with his apostles and after his passion, death, and resurrection, Jesus' apostles and disciples continued celebrating the paschal supper in obedience to the command of the Lord: "Do this in memory of me." The first Christians referred to this celebration as the "Supper of the

Lord" or the "Breaking of the Bread." The first references that we have of these celebrations are found in the Acts of the Apostles and in some of Saint Paul's letters. Obviously, in celebrating the Eucharist, the early Church did not have texts that contained the prayers and formats for the Mass such as we have today. The first Christians celebrated the "Supper of the Lord" with the format of the institution of the Eucharist that they knew by heart, and with prayers that the celebrant or the bishop recited in an improvised manner, following some pattern known by them based on traditional formats.[1]

Since there were no public buildings (churches) dedicated to worship, these relatively small groups of Christians celebrated in private homes. It is also important that we be aware that before the separation of Christianity and Judaism, after AD 70, the Christians did not see themselves as a separate religion from Judaism, but as Jews who had reached an acceptance of faith in Jesus of Nazareth as the awaited Messiah, as the Son of God. Consequently, being Jews, they attended the synagogue or the temple in Jerusalem. So they did not have separate churches but used their homes for the celebration of the Eucharist.

The celebration of the Eucharist in the early Church was family oriented and very informal. The Christians gathered on Sunday, or "the Day of the Lord," for a fraternal meal that they called agape. After the meal, they celebrated the "breaking of the bread," or "the Lord's Supper." There is no clear idea on what the Liturgy of the Word may have been

---

1   Klauser, Theodor, *A Short History of the Western Liturgy: An Account and Some Reflections.* Second edition, University Press: Oxford, 1979 (p. 9).

to the first communities, being that during the first years the canon of the New Testament did not yet exist. When the early Church spoke of the Scriptures, they were referring to the Old Testament or the Hebrew Scriptures. It is very probable that the first Christians attended the celebrations of the Word of the Lord in the synagogues or in the temple of Jerusalem. This does not discard the possibility that they themselves did not meditate on the Scriptures in their gatherings.

In the mid-second century, the Christians still did not have liturgical books. So a book did not exist with the format and prayers of the Mass. However, we have the written account of the rules and descriptions of the eucharistic celebration and other forms of praying and the celebrations of the sacrament during this period in the Church.

The first of these documents is the one known as the *Didache*. This document is also known as *Teachings of the Twelve Apostles*. It contains mainly disciplinary instructions for the life of the Christians. Some of its most important contents are liturgical directives.[2] Another of this kind of document is the *Didascalia*, which is known also as *The Catholic Teachings of the Twelve Apostles*. It was written at the beginning or the middle of the third century. Chapter twelve contains regulations for the liturgical celebrations and the places that were destined for worshiping. Just as the *Didache,* this document contains directives and not liturgical texts. Other manuscripts of the same type have survived and offer testimony of the liturgical practices of the Church during the second and third centuries.

---

2   Ibid, p. 12

But none of these texts gives us the formats that were used for the administration of the sacraments and, in particular, the Eucharist. Among others, we can name Justin the Martyr's *Apology* and the *Apostolic Constitutions*.[3]

The first document of the third century that the text provides, which was used during the eucharistic prayer or the Anaphora, is known as the Apostolic Tradition of Hippolytus.[4] It is important to note that even though this document gives us the basic structure of the eucharistic prayer, it is not yet considered a liturgical text used for the celebration of the Mass, which later would come to be a *Sacramentary* or a *Missal*.

During this period, worship in the Church remained hidden and not public since in these first centuries Christianity saw itself persecuted with short periods of relative peace and moments of pursuit that were sometimes very severe and at other times less severe. For this reason, the Church was confined to celebrating in private, domestic and not official. Gradually Christianity was growing and made itself present in all the corners of the Roman Empire. As a result, Rome realized that Christianity had become an entity that it would not be able to eliminate, as was its purpose at the beginning. Because of Christianity's growth, the emperor gave Christians freedom and then declared it the official religion of the empire. From being a persecuted and clandestine religion it became public and official, which would bring about an ecclesiastical and liturgical transformation.

---

3   Pecklers, Keith, *Liturgia en Contexto*, Paulinas Editorial: Caracas, 2007 (p. 52-3).
4   Ibid, p. 52

In the year 313, the Roman Emperor Constantine the Great promulgated the Edict of Milan, in which the Church received the freedom of worship from the Roman Empire. By 380, Christianity was recognized as the official religion of the empire. This liberty would allow Christian worship to begin developing fully. Worship began to take place in public buildings, namely the basilicas; additionally, the first liturgical books began appearing.

The first collection of liturgical texts are known by the Latin term *libelli*. This might be vaguely translated as small books that contain the prayers of the one who presides over the Mass, be it the bishop or the priest. These were written by different persons for their personal use, not intended as liturgical books but as models for other celebrants, and were passed from generation to generation. There were several collections of *libelli*. Gradually these private collections of prayers for the celebration of the Eucharist, other sacraments, and the *Liturgy of the Hours* became official books.

One of the liturgical books that developed in the Church through the centuries is the *Ordines Romani*, a book that originated in Rome and mainly contains instructions on how the solemn papal Masses should be celebrated. Other books include following: The *Sacramentary*, after the *Libellus*, came to be the main book for the celebration of the Mass and other sacraments; the *Lectionary* accompanies the *Sacramentary* in the celebration of the Eucharist, but it got to be the proper book for the Liturgy of the Word where the lectors proclaimed the word, the *Book of Gospels* came to be the book that the deacon uses to proclaim the Gospel; the *Antiphonal* came to be the book that contained the antiphons and responses of different liturgies, and it came to be the cantor's book in the choir. Other books that developed later in history were: the *Missal*, which appeared toward the end of the Middle Ages and came to replace the *Sacramentary*; the *Missal*, which joined in a single book the *Sacramentary*, the *Lectionary*, the *Book of Gospels* and the *Antiphonal*; the *Pontifical*, which has its origin in Rome as the *Book of Rites* for the papal liturgies and which much later was disseminated throughout Western Europe as the *Book of Rites* for the bishops; the *Book of Rites*, which was developed much later and which contains the rites for the celebrations of all the sacraments; the *Breviary*, which contains the different day and night prayers used by the religious and the clergy, and which is actually known as the *Liturgy of the Hours*.

The *Libellus*, using the singular Latin term, is the first liturgical book that was the transition between the improvisations of the Apostolic Era to what was becoming a truly liturgical book.

The *Libellus* came to be a type of pamphlet with some liturgical texts. In a way, it can be said that the *Libellus* became the ancestor of the *Sacramentary*.[5]

---

5   Palazzo, Eric, *A History of Liturgical Books From the Beginning to the Thirteenth Century*, The Liturgical Press: Collegeville, MN, 1998 (p.37).

Middle Ages to the Sixteenth Century

We can refer to the period of time that stretches from the fourth century to the Middle Ages as Antiquity, the Patristic Era, or as the time of the Fathers of the Church. During these years, there was great development in the liturgy with the participation of all the faithful in the liturgical celebrations. Also during this time, the Rite of Christian Initiation for Adults was at its peak.

Through the barbaric invasion from the north of Europe that prompted the fall of Rome, there came to Western Europe many drastic cultural and ecclesiastical changes. It was mainly during the Middle Ages that western Monastic culture was born and, with it, we also find the birth of the *scriptoria*. This came to be the term in Latin for the monastic shops where books were written, including the liturgical books that were used for the celebration of the different sacraments, especially the Mass.

A liturgical book called the *Sacramentary* appeared in the middle of the sixth century. This was the celebrant's principal book, and it contained the prayers, texts, and formats necessary for the priest, bishop or pope, or the order of the Mass with the canon: (eucharistic prayer), liturgical calendar, votive Masses and the rites for the celebration of other sacraments.[6] Continuing, we shall name some of the more important *Sacramentaries* of the Middle Ages, more or less in chronological order.

The *Leonine Sacramentary* was approximately composed in the middle of the sixth century. It is known by this name because it was mistakenly believed that Pope Leo I, who ruled

---

6   Ibid, p. 21

in the middle of the fifth century, had composed it.[7] One of the characteristics is that it is very rich in content, but it is not very practical since the majority of the material is very disorganized. Also it does not contain the celebrations for Lent and Easter, and you cannot find the canon. Its impracticality as a manual for the celebrants led to its replacement by another *Sacramentary*, the *Gelasiano*.

The *Gelasian Sacramentary* is known by this name because, by tradition, it was attributed to Pope Gelasius I (492–496). However, archeological investigations attested that this *Sacramentary* was actually composed in the middle of the seventh century. In contrast to the *Leonine Sacramentary*, the *Gelasian Sacramentary* is in every sense of the word a true liturgical book of Roman character.[8] This *Sacramentary* was very useful to the celebrants and for the dissemination of the Roman rite in Western Europe. Even though this *Sacramentary* was better organized than the *Leonine*, it still lacked the sobriety and simplicity that had been developed in the next *Sacramentary*, the *Gregorian*.

The *Gregorian Sacramentary* is believed to be the archetype of the *Sacramentary* compiled by Pope Saint Gregory the Great. It was put together during the first half of the seventh century. This *Sacramentary* was perfectly organized, which helped other Gregorian-type *Sacramentaries* to be derived from it. One of its main characteristics is the simplicity and solemnity that would come to be the style that would define a Roman liturgy.

---

7   Ibid, p. 40-1
8   Ibid, p. 45

In the latter part of the Middle Ages, from the tenth century until the Renaissance (sixteenth century), a transition of the liturgical books was achieved, due to changes in the way the Mass was celebrated. Some ministries that other ministers performed were assigned to the celebrant; the multiplication of Masses and private Masses were also put into use in which the celebrant celebrating alone fulfilled all the ministries of the Mass. Thus, it was necessary to unite these books into one book: the *Lectionary*, the *Book of the Gospels* (the readings) and the parts which were sung, on occasion with the musical notations, in what before was the *Sacramentary*. All of the necessary elements for the celebration of the Mass were united into only one book, the *Missal*.[9]

The development of the *Missal* was extremely important to the celebration of the Mass in the late Middle Ages. The people did not speak Latin anymore, so they could not participate in the Mass nor understand it. There were no lay ministers to assist in the celebration, nor permanent deacons, nor a choir. Without the participation of all these elements, it was believed that it would be more practical that all the books—the *Sacramentary*, the *Lectionary*, the *Book of Gospels* and the *Antiphony*—become condensed into one—the *Missal*.

It was then that the Mass became a celebration led by the priest. The people went to hear Mass, and while the priest prayed the Mass, the lay people prayed other prayers: the rosary, novenas, or other popular devotions. The lay people received holy Communion. Instead of a sacramental Commu-

---

9   Ibid, p. 107-10.

nion, a spiritual Communion was developed through a great devotion to the Blessed Sacrament through adoration. From here, the great Corpus Christi procession was born, that is, the solemnity of the body and blood of Christ.

During the Middle Ages, with the distancing of participation in the Mass by the lay people, magical and superstitious elements were attributed to the Eucharist. Participation in the Mass was no longer seen as important as the sheer multiplication of Masses. There were many abuses on the part of the clergy in regards to the stipends for celebrating Mass. This liturgical, theological, and moral decline of the Church continued in varying degrees until the sixteenth century.

From the Council of Trent to the Second Vatican Council

At the beginning of the sixteenth century, Martin Luther's denouncing of what he perceived to be abuses in the Church and in the liturgy led to the Protestant Reformation. From there sprang a great gamut of Protestant reformers who followed in his footsteps, such as Ulrich Zwingli, Martin Bucer, John Calvin, and Thomas Cranmer. The Catholic Church saw it was necessary not only to answer the challenges that were presented by the Protestant Reformation, but also the need to put in order several chaotic and abusive situations that needed to be corrected. This reaction is known as the Counter-Reformation. It became imperative to convoke an ecumenical council that would be known as the Council of Trent.

The Council of Trent, begun in 1545, gave birth to a new series of reforms in the Church, which would have direct repercussions in the liturgy, such as a centralization, uniformity, and rigidness in the liturgical practices, especially in the celebration of the Mass. As part of these reforms, the *Roman Missal* was introduced publicly in 1570. Known as the *Pope Pius V Missal*, it would be used throughout the Church in the Latin rite and any other non-Roman Catholic rite that was more than two hundred years old. This *Missal* with all of its formulas and rubrics would prevail from the end of the sixteenth century until the introduction of the *Pope Paul VI Missal* in 1970 following the Second Vatican Council liturgical reforms. Contrary to the Protestant reformers who had implemented their liturgies in the vernacular instead of Latin, the Council of Trent decided to continue with Latin as the only language with which the Church would celebrate liturgies. This was in spite of the fact that there were some bishops who pleaded that the Mass have several parts in the common language which was spoken by the people in different places. They pleaded that, at the very least, the Word of God should be proclaimed in the vernacular. However, for some of the more conservative bishops, this appeared to them to be a very Protestant practice.

Mainly there were three concrete results of liturgical character in the reforms of this Council: the renewal of the *Roman Breviary*, publicized in 1568, that is to say, the *Liturgy of the Hours*, the book that governs the different Church prayers and the hours of the day during which to pray; *Pius V Roman Missal*; and in 1588 the Sacred Congregation of the Rites. This body would come to be the one that would govern the liturgical life of the Church and which was the predecessor of what would be today, after the Second Vatican Council, the Congregation for Divine Worship and the Discipline of the Sacraments. The *Pius V Missal* established the rubrics or norms of how the Mass was to be celebrated after the Council of Trent to stop the abuses and maintain uniformity in the celebration of the Mass. For this reason the norms that in the past were useful as a guide were changed to rubrics of a moral and juridical type that determined whether the Mass was valid or invalid. What was descriptive was converted to obligatory norms.[10] This is the normative Mass of the Latin or Roman Rite of the Catholic Church until the Paul VI Mass after Vatican II, and is known as the Tridentine Mass. In this Mass, which some people still remember before Vatican II, is celebrated in Latin with the altar against the apse of the Church: the priest celebrated the Eucharist with his back to the people. The sanctuary divided the priest from the community by a banister called the Communion rail, in which few of the communicants would receive it kneeling.

The *Trenton Roman Missal*, which would come to govern the Roman or Latin rite of the Catholic Church during four centuries, had several revisions during that time. The last was the one that Pope John XXIII made in 1962 and which came to be the current *Missal* that is used for the celebration in the extraordinary form; in other words, the Tridentine Mass in Latin. Some of its principal aspects are worthy of mention. There was a purification of saints' feast days that had grown more

---

10 Pecklers, Keith F., *The Genius of the Roman Rite: On the Reception and Implementation of the New Missal.* Liturgical Press: Collegeville, MN, 2009, (p.19).

important than the Sunday celebrations and other Christological feasts and solemnities from the liturgical calendar, including Advent, Lent, and Easter.

The *Missal* was unified into one book since there were several different *Missals* which were being used in different dioceses. The importance of private Masses was diminished and the celebration of the Mass as a community was highlighted. In addition, preference was given to the solemn Mass instead of the simple Mass that was known as the *Misa Breve*, or the Brief Mass. During these centuries, great emphasis was given to the total adherence to the rubrics or rules in the *Missal* that indicated how the Mass should be celebrated. Thus the Council of Trent was able to gain uniformity and rigidness that would characterize the celebration of the Mass and the liturgy in general for four centuries.

The Second Vatican Council

After the death of Pope Pius XII in 1958, the new pope, John XXIII, convoked the Second Vatican Council in 1959, a few months after his election. Due to his advanced age, Pope John XXIII died shortly after having begun the council. As a result, the responsibility of continuing and concluding the council would fall on the shoulders of Pope Paul VI. One of the tasks of the council was that of updating the Church before the reality of the modern world of the twentieth century. In Italian, this is called *agornamiento*. Among all the pastoral affairs that the council had to deal with, liturgy was the first. Thus the Constitution on the Sacred Liturgy (*Sarosanctum*

Concilium) was the first to be approved by the council fathers. With a majority of votes, it was approved on December 4, 1963.

After the promulgation of the Constitution on the Sacred Liturgy, a group was immediately formed, *Concilium*, which took charge in preparing the implementation of the changes in the liturgy dictated by the constitution. These changes included the revision of the rites of the sacraments, the preparation of a new *Lectionary* (which would later be translated into the vernacular languages), and the revision of the *Liturgy of the Hours* or *Divine Office*. All these documents had to be prepared in Latin and later translated into the vernacular languages. However, implementing the changes to the celebration of the Mass would be one of the most important and urgent tasks for the members of *Concilium*. This signified that a new *Roman Missal* had to be created that reflected the liturgical renewal of the Second Vatican Council.

The 1970 *Roman Missal of Paul VI*

One of the principal directives of the Constitution on the Sacred Liturgy was that while the faithful participate in the liturgy, especially the celebration of the Eucharist, that the participation be conscious, full, and active. For the creation of a new *Missal*, this directive would have several consequences. Changes would have to be made to the liturgical language so that the people could participate in a language they understood and spoke, not only to understand the different formats and prayers, but also to be able to answer and pray together with the celebrant. If the celebrant says, "Let us pray," then we have to pray together; if the celebrant invites us to give thanks to the Lord in the format of a dialogue in the preface, "let us give thanks to the Lord, Our God," the faithful not only are united in giving thanks, but they are also completely conscious of why thanks are given to God.

In 1964, formal commissions were established in the different national conferences of bishops for the translation of liturgical texts in the language of each country. The International Commission on English in the Liturgy (ICEL) was formed, not only for one specific English-speaking episcopal conference, but for all the English-speaking countries. The directives that would be suggested for the translation of the liturgical texts from Latin to other languages were published in an official document called the Instructions of *Comme le Prévoit*. This document was originally written in French and thus the title was kept in the same language.

The changes to the liturgy not only had to do with the language. In order to facilitate full, conscious, and active participation, it was necessary to make some changes to the rite. For example, so that the faithful might have better access to the eucharistic celebration, it was necessary to remove the altar that was attached to the wall so that the priest could celebrate the eucharistic liturgy facing the people. To allow for the participation of the faithful in the proclamation of the Word of the Lord, the readings had to be removed from the *Missal* and a *Lectionary* and a *Books of Gospels* created.

There were only two readings in the *Trenton Missal*; namely, the Epistle and the Gospel with only an annual cycle. However, in the liturgical renewal of the Second Vatican Council, three readings were introduced for the Liturgy of the Word at Sunday Masses and solemnities and three annual cycles. Two readings were kept for weekday Masses with two annual cycles for the first reading and one annual cycle for the Gospel. Three new eucharistic prayers, or anaphoras, were created, since the *Trenton Missal* only had one, the first, which is also known as the Roman Canon. Also, the rite of Peace was reintroduced into the Liturgy of the Eucharist. The Prayer of the Faithful was restored to be proclaimed after the recitation of the creed, in order to serve as a link between the Liturgy of the Word and the Liturgy of the Eucharist. Restored also, in all its beauty, richness, and symbolism, was the celebration of the paschal Vigil as part of the paschal Triduum during Holy Week. Having these and many other details in mind, the new *Roman Missal* was created. This missal is known as the *Paul VI Missal*, since he was the reigning pope when it was produced. We must remember that the *Missal* was composed in Latin, which would come to be the basic text (typical text or *edition tipica* in Latin). This text was published in 1969. It is the Latin text of the *Missal* which was then translated into the diverse languages of the Catholic world.

By 1970, in less than a year's time, the majority of the national episcopal conferences had already translated the new *Missal* to their own vernacular language.

The First Edition of the *Roman Missal* in 1974

Between the first publication of the *Paul VI Missal* and the first edition (1969–1974) there was a very short span of barely five years. And, between the approval of the Constitution on the Sacred Liturgy and the publication of the *Paul VI Roman Missal* (1963–1969) there also was a very short span of time. In this six-year period, another liturgical work of greater importance was produced. There was a sense of urgency in implementing the liturgical reforms from the council, particularly the *Roman Missal*. This urgency to have the new text of the celebration of the Eucharist gave way to the realization that revisions had to be made to the original text in the typical edition, the Latin one (*editio tipica*), as in the vernacular versions. In this last one, we must take into account that there was no experience for translating the texts for liturgical or ritual use in almost the entire history of the Catholic Church. From the fourth century until the twentieth century, the only language used in the liturgy was Latin. It was in 1974 that the need was seen to have the first edition in Latin of the *Roman Missal*. Subsequently, the corresponding translations were made in all the other languages. It is precisely through this experience that the development of criteria and rules for the translation of liturgical and ritual texts emerge.

The Second Edition of the *Roman Missal* in 1985

The first edition survived a bit longer than the original text of the 1969 *Roman Missal*. It lasted eleven years, from 1974 to 1985. The liturgy is a living and dynamic organism that is celebrated by living beings who respond to the divine initiative to be gathered by the same God in order to be sanctified and redeemed through the merits of the passion, death, and resurrection of his Son, Jesus Christ. In our constant effort to improve the way we relate to God through the liturgy, the need was seen to revise the *Roman Missal* and to make a second edition.

However, this second edition never was finished in English, since the revision process was very slow and controversial. The third English edition arrived before the second English edition was ever completed. This second edition was finalized in other major languages, including the edition in Spanish. Thus, Spanish, French, Italian, Portuguese and other languages published their missals during the 1980s. Later, in 1991, other Anaphoras called "Eucharistic Prayers for Various Needs and Occasions" were added.[11] These Anaphoras come as part of the appendix of the *Roman Missal* in English. They are known as the Eucharistic Prayers for Children and for Reconciliation.

---

11 *The Genius of the Roman Rite*, (p.56).
12 Chupungco, Anscar J., *What, Then, Is Liturgy? Musings and Memoir*. Liturgical Press: Collegeville, MN, 2010, (p. 189).

The 2002 Third Edition of the *Roman Missal*

In 2001, Pope John Paul II decreed the document *Liturgiam Authenticam,* in which new directives were given to govern the translation of texts for the use in liturgy from Latin to other languages. These directions would come to replace those given in the 1999 *Comme le Prévoit* document.[12] After the promulgation of *Liturgiam Authenticam*, the third edition of the *Roman Missal* followed a year later in 2002. It was to be expected that with the new directives for liturgical translations the *Missal* would have to be revised so that the new translations would conform to the new directives. In the following section, we shall formulate a series of questions that will give us a better idea of what changes the third edition of the *Roman Missal* will have.

THE NEW TRANSLATION BASED ON THE THIRD EDITION OF THE *ROMAN MISSAL*

Why a new translation?

Throughout the history of Christianity, the formats and prayers that have been used for divine worship have been changing and evolving, in some eras at a more accelerated manner than others, and at other times, at a slower pace. In this third edition of the *Paul VI Missal*, the rules of the game changed. The changes are neither arbitrary nor superficial. The liturgical experts at the beginning of the third millennium have a very different point of view about what is most important in the translation of liturgical texts than did the pioneers in such translations at the beginning of the liturgical renewal following the Second Vatican Council.

This change is the result of years of experience in liturgical translation which did not exist at the beginning of the liturgical renewal. These beginnings set the foundations for the rites in the vernacular or national languages. Upon these foundations, the Church has built something new: the third edition of the *Roman Missal*.

Later on, we will take a closer look at the differences

between *Liturgiam Autenticam* and *Comme le Prévoit*. For now, suffice it to say that the first document in the seventies, *Comme le Prévoit*, was governed by the principle called "dynamic equivalency," which was not inevitably a literal translation, but a translation that gives us the main idea of what the translated and original text says. On the other hand, the directives dictated by the document *Liturgiam Authenticam* require "formal equivalency." This demands a translation that is more literal and adheres to the original text. This is the principle which guides the translation of the third edition of the *Paul VI Roman Missal*.

Who Makes the Translations?

Each country has an Episcopal Conference, that is, a conference formed by all the bishops of one country. Each conference forms a commission that is in change of the translation of liturgical books. In the case of English, instead of each English-speaking country having a commission, there is an international commission called the International Commission on English in the Liturgy, or ICEL. These commissions, be they national or international, have the job of translating the texts from Latin to their proper language for the liturgy; in this case, the *Roman Missal*. Once these commissions have completed the translation, the translated text is presented to the bishops of the national conference to be approved, and if the bishops approve the text, then it is presented to the Congregation for Divine Worship and the Discipline of the Sacraments for a final approval, which in Latin is called a *recognitio*. If the commission for translating is international, then each of the countries represented in this commission has to approve the translated text, and each country, separately, has to present the text to Rome for a *recognitio*. As the translation in English for the third edition of the *Roman Missal* made by ICEL caused a bit of controversy, another English-speaking international committee was formed by bishops and specialists in liturgy called *Vox Clara*. This committee was in charge of reviewing the texts translated by ICEL. This revision of the text was presented to the English-speaking Episcopal Conferences for their approval and finally to Rome for the final *recognitio*.

What Changes Will the New Translation Have?

As was mentioned at the beginning, the *Missal* in Spanish will not have as many changes to the parts of the assembly. The main changes will have to do with the presider's parts. For example, new translations will be done for the prayer that the priest says after the Gloria, the Opening Prayer, the Prayer over the Gifts, and the Prayer after Communion for the entire Liturgical Year, including Sundays, the different liturgical seasons (Advent, Christmas, Lent, and Easter), the solemnities and the feasts of the Blessed Mother and the Saints. Also, the formula for consecration will change.

The present translation for consecrating the host says:

Priest: Take this, all of you, and eat it:
            this is my body,
            which will be given up for you.

[Then continues with the Chalice]

Priest: Take this, all of you, and drink from it:
            this is the cup of my blood,
            the blood of the new and everlasting covenant.
            It will be shed for you and **for all men**
            so that sins may be forgiven.
            Do this in memory of me.

The new translation will change "for all men" to "for many." The new verbiage for the consecration will be as follows:

Priest: Take this, all of you, and eat from it,
            this is my body,
            which will be given up for you.

[Then continues with the Chalice]

Priest: Take this, all of you, and drink from it,
            this is the cup of my Blood,
            the blood of the new and everlasting covenant.
            It will be shed for you and **for many**
            so that sins may be forgiven.
            Do this in memory of me.

The majority of the Latin American countries do not use "vosotros" (thou) but "usted" (you). This is why almost all the Latin American Conferences, including the translation in Spanish for use in the United States, has asked Rome to allow the use of "usted" instead of "vosotros." Rome has allowed this change not only in the formula for the consecration, but in all the formats that contain "vosotros." The change from "for all men" to "for many" has to do with the text in Latin that used the words *pro multis*, and which can be translated as "for all or for many." Rome has given preference to a translation that is both more literal, and is the word that Jesus used in the Last Supper in the Gospels of Matthew (26:28) and Mark (14:24).

The changes in the English *Roman Missal* have been more copious and more radical. Continuing, we have some of the principal changes to the assembly's parts in English in chronological order in the Ordinary of the Mass. Please note: In general, on the left-hand pages we have the present text, and on the right-hand pages we have the new translation.

✠ THE GREETING

Old

Priest:　The Lord be with you.
People:　**And also with you.**

✠ THE GREETING

Priest: The Lord be with you.
People: **And with your spirit.**

The response to the greeting, "The Lord be with you" is, "And also with you." However, in the new translation, the response will change to, "And with your spirit" since that is the literal response in the Latin typical edition. Why this response? This response is traditionally taken from the conclusions of the following Letters of Saint Paul: Galatians, Philippians, 2 Timothy, and Philemon. In ritual gatherings where a meal was shared, the Jews of Jesus' time also used the same greeting, and the response was, "and with your spirit." In the new translation, this response is preferred because it expresses the desire that the Holy Spirit be present in all the assembly, but above all, with the man who presides over the community prayer, the priest.

✠ THE PENITENTIAL RITE

I confess to almighty God,
and to you, my brothers and sisters,
that I have **sinned through my own fault**
in my thoughts and in my words,
in what I have done,
and in what I have failed to do;
and I ask blessed Mary, ever virgin,
all the angels and saints,
and you, my brothers and sisters,
to pray for me to the Lord our God.

Priest: **Lord, we have sinned against you:**
Lord, have mercy.
People: **Lord, have mercy.**
Priest: **Lord, show us your mercy and love.**
People: And grant us your salvation.

☩ THE PENITENTIAL RITE

New

I confess to almighty God
and to you, my brothers and sisters,
that I have **greatly sinned**
in my thoughts and in my words,
in what I have done
and in what I have failed to do,
through my fault,
through my fault,
through my most grievous fault;
therefore I ask blessed Mary, ever-Virgin,
all the Angels and Saints,
and you, my brothers and sisters,
to pray for me to the Lord our God.

Priest: **Have mercy on us, O Lord.**
People: **For we have sinned against you.**
Priest: **Show us, O Lord, your mercy.**
People: And grant us your salvation.

The "I confess," or as it is known in Latin, the *Confiteor,* can be seen above. The revised prayer does not substantially change, but has added parts that the prayer in Latin contains. This is in accordance with the new rules for translating the liturgical texts that state the translation must be as close as possible to the Latin text. What was added is: "…that I have greatly sinned…" and "through my fault, through my fault, through my most grievous fault.…" This better expresses the gravity of our sins and our sincere sorrow. It also helps us avoid taking the consequences of our sinful actions so lightly.

✠ THE GLORIA

Old

Glory to God in the highest,
and **peace to his people on earth.**
Lord God, heavenly King,
almighty God and Father,
    we worship you, we give you thanks,
    we praise you for your glory.
Lord Jesus Christ, only Son of the Father,
Lord God, Lamb of God,
you take away the sin of the world:
    have mercy on us;
you are seated at the right hand of the Father:
    receive our prayer.
For you alone are the Holy One,
you alone are the Lord,
you alone are the Most High,
    Jesus Christ, with the Holy Spirit,
    in the glory of God the Father. Amen.

✛ THE GLORIA

New

Glory to God in the highest,
and **on earth peace to people of good will.**
We praise you, we bless you, we adore you,
we glorify you, we give you thanks **for your great glory,**
Lord God, heavenly King, **O God, almighty Father.**
Lord Jesus Christ, **Only Begotten Son,**
Lord God, Lamb of God,
Son of the Father,
you take away the **sins** of the world,
　　have mercy on us;
you take away the sins of the world,
　　receive our prayer;
you are seated at the right hand of the Father,
　　have mercy on us.
For you alone are the Holy One,
　　you alone are the Lord,
you alone are the Most High,
　　Jesus Christ, with the Holy Spirit,
　　in the glory of God the Father. Amen.

Once again, with the Gloria, the changes have to do with the need to adhere more closely to the Latin text. The present translation says: "And peace to his people on earth." The new translation, which is a more literal translation of the Latin, says: "And peace to the people of good will." This translation is not only closer to the text in Latin, but has a more direct connection to the passage of the Gospel of Saint Luke (2:14) when the angels appeared to the shepherds in Bethlehem announcing God's peace and the birth of the child Jesus.

☩ THE GOSPEL'S RESPONSE

Old

Deacon (or Priest): A reading from the holy Gospel according to N.
People: **Glory to you, Lord.**

☩ THE GOSPEL'S RESPONSE

New

Deacon (or Priest): A reading from the holy Gospel according to N.

People: **Glory to you, O Lord.**

To the final response of the proclamation of the Gospel the expression "O" was simply added to "Lord." "Glory to you, O Lord." There is no better explanation for this than the one that the new translation is closest to the typical text in Latin.

✛ THE NICENE-CONSTANTINOPOLITAN CREED

Old

We believe in one God,
the Father, the Almighty,
maker of heaven and earth,
of all that is seen and unseen.
We believe in one Lord, Jesus Christ,
the only Son of God,
eternally begotten of the Father,
God from God, Light from Light,
true God from true God,
begotten, not made,
one in Being with the Father.
Through him all things were made.
For us men and for our salvation
he came down from heaven:
by the power of the Holy Spirit
he was born of the Virgin Mary,
and became man.
For our sake he was crucified under Pontius Pilate;
he suffered, died, and was buried.
On the third day he rose again
in **fulfillment of** the Scriptures;
he ascended into heaven
and is seated at the right hand of the Father.

He will come again in glory
to judge the living and the dead,
and his kingdom will have no end.

We believe in the Holy Spirit,
the Lord, the giver of life, who proceeds from the Father and the Son.
With the Father and the Son
he is worshiped and glorified.
He has spoken through the Prophets.

We believe in one holy catholic
and apostolic Church**.**
We acknowledge one baptism
for the forgiveness of sins**.**
We look for the
resurrection of the dead**,**
and the life of the world to come. Amen.

✠ THE NICENE-CONSTANTINOPOLITAN CREED

New

I believe in one God, the Father almighty,
maker of heaven and earth,
of all **things visible and invisible.**

I believe in one Lord Jesus Christ,
the Only **Begotten** Son of God,
born of the Father **before all ages.**

God from God, Light from Light,
true God from true God,
begotten, not made,
consubstantial with the Father;
through him all things were made.
For us men and for our salvation
he came down from heaven,
and by the Holy Spirit
was incarnate of the Virgin Mary, and became man.
For our sake he was crucified under Pontius Pilate,
he suffered death and was buried,
and rose again on the third day
in **accordance with** the Scriptures.
He ascended into heaven
and is seated at the right hand of the Father.

He will come again in glory
to judge the living and the dead
and his kingdom will have no end.

I believe in the Holy Spirit,
the Lord, the giver of life,
who proceeds from the Father and the Son,
who with the Father and the Son
is adored and glorified,
who has spoken through the prophets.

I believe in one, holy,
catholic and apostolic Church.
I confess one Baptism
for the forgiveness of sins
and I look forward to the resurrection of the dead
and the life of the world to come. Amen.

The creed which we usually profess at Sunday Masses and on solemnities is recognized as the Nicene-Constantinopolitan Creed because it was formatted during the Councils of Nicea and Constantinople. The main change that we see in this format is that the person changes from the first person plural to the first person singular. In other words, it changes from "we believe" to "I believe." This is primarily due to two reasons. The first is that "credo" in Latin means "I believe" and not "we believe"; and the second is that even though the profession of faith is done in a public forum, it is a very personal act. There are two other changes that we can see in the bold letters and that give us a more precise translation of the text in Latin.

☩ THE APOSTLES' CREED

Old

I believe in God, the Father almighty,
creator of heaven and earth.

I believe in Jesus Christ,
his only Son, our Lord.
He was conceived by
the power of the Holy Spirit
and born of the Virgin Mary.
He suffered under Pontius Pilate,
was crucified, died, and was buried.
He descended **to the dead.**
On the third day he rose again.

He ascended into heaven,
and is seated at the right hand
of the Father.
He will come **again** to judge
the living and the dead.

I believe in the Holy Spirit,
the holy catholic Church,
the communion of saints,
the forgiveness of sins,
the resurrection of the body,
and **the** life everlasting. Amen.

✟ THE APOSTLES' CREED

New

I believe in God, the Father almighty,
Creator of heaven and earth**,**
and in Jesus Christ,
his only Son, our Lord,
who was conceived by
the Holy Spirit,
born of the Virgin Mary,
suffered under Pontius Pilate,
was crucified, died and was buried**;**
he descended **into hell;**
on the third day he rose again
from the dead;

he ascended into heaven,
and is seated at the right hand
of **God** the Father **almighty;**
from there he will come to judge
the living and the dead.

I believe in the Holy Spirit,
the holy catholic Church,
the communion of saints,
the forgiveness of sins,
the resurrection of the body,
and life everlasting. Amen.

The Apostles' Creed had minor changes to it. It is clear that the new text uses a language that is more precise and adheres more closely to the Latin.

The most important change here is in the present translation of the English, which says that Jesus, after his death, descended to the place of the dead. But in Latin it says, "descended into hell." In this case, the Latin noun does not mean hell, the place of eternal damnation. Instead, it refers to a netherworld for those who had died before Jesus and who were awaiting their salvation. Jesus Christ descends there to rescue them and to carry them with him to heaven and to their salvation.

☩ THE *SUSCIPIAT DOMINUS*

(May the Lord accept the sacrifice at your hands…)

Old

May the Lord accept the sacrifice
at your hands
for the praise and glory of his name, for our good,
and the good of all his Church.

✠ THE *SUSCIPIAT DOMINUS*

(May the Lord accept the sacrifice at your hands…)

New

May the Lord accept the sacrifice
at your hands
for the praise and glory of his name, for our good
and the good of all his **holy** Church.

In response to the priest's invitation to pray that the sacrifice that is going to be offered be more acceptable to God, the response of the assembly has only one change. We add a classifying adjective to the word Church: holy.

It is good to refer to the Church as holy since it has been sanctified by Christ's own sacrifice, which we are preparing to offer. We are not a holy Church through our merits, but through the merits of the passion, death, and resurrection of our Lord Jesus Christ, the paschal mystery that we celebrate when we offer the holy sacrifice of the Mass.

✠ THE DIALOGUE OF THE PREFACE

Old

Priest: The Lord be with you.

People: **And also with you.**

Priest: Lift up your hearts.

People: We lift them up to the Lord.

Priest: Let us give thanks to the Lord our God.

People: **It is right to give him thanks and praise.**

✛ THE DIALOGUE OF THE PREFACE

New

Priest: The Lord be with you.

People: **And with your spirit.**

Priest: Lift up your hearts.

People: We lift them up to the Lord.

Priest: Let us give thanks to the Lord our God.

People: **It is right and just.**

The eucharistic prayer begins with the preface, and the preface with a dialogue. The last response of this dialogue is the invitation: "Let us give thanks to the Lord, our God," and the response is, "It is right to give him thanks and praise." The new text of the third edition is: "It is right and just." Once more, this is in response to the ruling that the translation be more accurate to the text in Latin. This expresses our duty as a Church, and it is precisely what we do when we celebrate every liturgy; namely, give thanks to our God for the ways he blesses us and gives us love and our salvation through Jesus Christ our Lord. That is why it is right and just to give thanks to God at all times and in all places.

✠ THE *SANCTUS*
(Holy, holy, holy...)

Old

Holy, holy, holy Lord, God of **power and might.**
Heaven and earth are full of your glory.
Hosanna in the highest.
Blessed is he who comes
in the name of the Lord.
Hosanna in the highest.

✛ THE *SANCTUS*

(Holy, holy, holy...)

New

Holy, Holy, Holy **Lord God of hosts.**
Heaven and earth are full of your glory.
Hosanna in the highest.
Blessed is he who comes
in the name of the Lord.
Hosanna in the highest.

> The hymn of the Holy, which prepares us for the main part of the eucharistic prayer, the consecration, has only one change. The present text says: "God of power and might" and the new text is translated as: "Lord God of hosts." The original text in Latin defines God as "Sabaoth," which is a Hebrew term and refers to a God who leads his army of angels in the battle against evil. As such, the closest English expression that captures this meaning would be, "God of hosts."

✠ THE MYSTERY OF FAITH

(The Memorial Acclamation)

Old

Priest: **Let us proclaim
the mystery of faith:**

People:

A –   Christ has died, Christ is risen,
        Christ will come again.

or B – Dying you destroyed our death,
        rising you restored our life.
        Lord Jesus, come in glory.

or C – When we eat this bread
        and drink this cup,
        we proclaim your death,
        Lord Jesus,
        until you come **in glory.**

or D – **Lord,** by your cross
        and resurrection,
        you have set us free.
        You are the Savior of the World.

✝ THE MYSTERY OF FAITH
(The Memorial Acclamation)

New

Priest: **The mystery of faith.**
People:

A — **We proclaim your Death,**
   O Lord,
   and profess your Resurrection
   until you come again.

or B — When we eat this Bread
   and drink this Cup,
   we proclaim your Death,
   O Lord,
   until you come **again.**

or C — **Save us, Savior of the world,**
   for by your Cross
   and Resurrection
   you have set us free.

In the Memorial Acclamation of the English Mass, the priest invites the gathered community to a proclamation of the mystery of faith. However, the new translation teaches that the mystery of faith, at this moment, is not a proclamation, but an acclamation, and that the act of inviting to proclaim distracts the celebrant from the prayer. Let us not forget that the priest, in the name of the assembly, is in prayer with God during the eucharistic prayer. Therefore, the new translation will not be an invitation, but an acclamation followed by an acclamation response by the assembly. The response of the assembly changes a bit since the new translation is more faithful to the Latin text. The response, "Christ has died, Christ is risen, Christ will come again" is omitted. This is done because there is no equivalent text in the original Latin and also because it is more a proclamation of faith than a prayer.

✠ THE *AGNUS DEI*
(This is the Lamb of God...)

Old

Priest: **This is** the Lamb of God
who takes away
the sins of the world.
Happy are those **who are** called
to **his** supper.

All: Lord, I am not worthy
to receive you,
but only say the word
and **I** shall be healed.

✠ THE *AGNUS DEI*
(Behold the Lamb of God...)

New

Priest: **Behold** the Lamb of God**,**
behold him who takes away
the sins of the world.
Blessed are those called
to **the** supper **of the Lamb.**

All: Lord, I am not worthy
that you should enter under my roof,
but only say the word
and **my soul** shall be healed.

In the actual format of the Lamb of God, the priest says: "This is the Lamb of God." However, the new translation is both closer to the original text and also more faithful to the passage in the Gospel of Saint John (1:29) in which he makes the reference: "Behold the Lamb of God." So the new translation will be: "Behold the Lamb of God, behold him who takes away the sins of the world." Instead of saying, "Lord, I am not worthy to receive you," the response of the assembly will be, "Lord, I am not worthy that you should enter under my roof." This is another way of saying, "I am not worthy that you should enter my house," like the response in Spanish. Why this change? Once again, this will make the translation more faithful to the original Latin. At the same time, it better reflects the Gospel passages that make this reference (Matthew 8:8 and Luke 7:6). In the Scripture texts, the centurion asks Jesus to heal his servant. Then, when he sees Jesus walking toward his house to heal the servant, the centurion explains, "I am not worthy to have you enter under my roof...."

These are some of the more important changes, above all in what concerns the responses of the assembly. There are other changes that have to do more with the prayers and formulas for the priest who is presiding at the Eucharist.

WHAT ARE
SOME OF THE CRITERIA
THAT WILL BE USED
FOR THE LITURGICAL
TRANSLATIONS?

Since the latter part of the 1960s, the Catholic Church began using a new format for celebrating the liturgy. Part of this was celebrating the liturgies in other languages, and not only in Latin, as had been done in previous centuries. This new experience required that the Church undertake a task that had not been previously done; namely, translate Latin texts into the vernacular languages for liturgical use. As a result, it became necessary to offer criteria and rules for the translation of Latin liturgical texts into the diverse languages of the Catholic world. The first of these documents was *Comme le Prévoit.*

Comme le Prévoit, 1969

The document *Comme le Prévoit* was published by the *Consilium* in 1969. It contains the rules for the translation of liturgical texts, and its title is maintained in French, since that is the language it was originally written in. It was written during a time of liturgical experimentation in the Church.

The basic principle that governs this document is what is called "dynamic equivalency." This means that the main emphasis in the translation is not on a literal translation or on adhering to the original text, but better yet, it gives more importance to the communication. We have to discuss the true significance of the text in its entirety and not focus on individual words. It is also stated that the liturgical translations should be faithful to the art of communication in all its aspects.[13] It speaks of the importance of taking into account both the historical and cultural context of the language into which one is translating. This means that liturgical texts should be translated dynamically so that they are understandable by the assembly that is gathered to celebrate.[14] One of the priorities of this document is to facilitate the full, conscious, and active participation of the faithful in the liturgy, even if it means sacrificing the beauty and the richness of the ancient liturgical texts in Latin.[15] There are several aspects that have to be taken into account when you make a translation, keeping in mind the principle of "dynamic equivalence": the same message in its totality, the audience to whom the translation is directed, and one must keep in mind the manner of expression.[16]

---

13 *The Genius of the Roman Rite*, p. 54.

14 Ibid.

15 Chupungco, p. 190.

16 Ibid, p. 192.

This document was written by the Congregation for the Divine Cult and the Discipline of the Sacraments in Rome in 2001, which happened to be one year prior to the publication of the third edition of the *Roman Missal* in Latin. The publication of this document coincides with a period that surpasses the time of experimentation in the translation of liturgical texts from Latin to the vernacular languages. At this time, much focus is given to the question of the translation of liturgical texts.

The principle of "dynamic equivalency," presented in the document *Comme le Prévoit* as a rule for the translation of texts for liturgical use, would become obsolete with the publication of the new document, *Liturgiam Authenticam.* From 2001 on, the rules for translating liturgical documents would come from this last document, with a different operating principle than was used in *Comme le Prévoit.* This new operating principle is that of "formal equivalence" or "formal correspondence."

"Formal equivalence" functions very differently from "dynamic equivalence." The translation of liturgical texts using formal equivalence has to give priority to a more literal translation, faithful and doctrinally correct, from the Latin into the vernacular languages. This document also places new restrictions on the commissions dedicated to the translation of the liturgical texts. The commissions have to obtain the *nihil obstat* before working on any translation of a liturgical type.[17]

---

17 *The Genius of the Roman Rite,* p. 61.

Another of the requirements that *Liturgiam Authenticam* demands is to avoid the tendencies to manipulate "psychologically" and the "ideological influences."[18] Perhaps this is in response to the efforts by some members of the translating commission to include in their translations a more inclusive language in which all kinds of readers do not feel excluded by the terms used in the translation. In the year 2007, the Congregation for the Divine Worship and the Discipline of the Sacraments published another document which would come to reinforce the principles given for *Liturgiam Authenticam*. Some comments about this document are offered in what follows.

Ratio Translationis, 2007

As was previously mentioned, in 2001, new rules were given for how to translate liturgical texts from Latin to other languages in general. These rules may vary from one language to another according to the nature and rules of each language. That is why, in 2007, the Congregation for Divine Worship and the Discipline of the Sacraments promulgated another instruction for the translation of liturgical texts from Latin into English. The purpose of the document is to provide a basic guide for those conferences that may be in charge of the translation in English. This document was made under the guidance of the *Vox Clara* committee, which was made up of bishops and experts on the liturgy from different English-speaking countries.

---

18   Ibid, p. 62.

This document, *Ratio Translationis for the English Language*, basically contains three parts and some appendices. The first part speaks of the basic presuppositions for an authentic translation of the Latin or Roman rite. This includes an explanation of the significance of the liturgical language which has to have its proper character and style since this is the language that is used to direct ourselves to God. It also offers the following seven principles for the language of the Liturgical Roman rite: It is Trinitarian, eschatological, biblical, patristic, direct and compact, pedagogical, and comprises each person in its totality. The second part offers us the principles of translation for the Liturgy of the Roman rite. This second part tells us that the identity and the united expression of the Roman rite have to be preserved; that priority has to be given to the biblical language and expression; that the translations of the typical editions (Latin) should avoid paraphrasing expressions; that the vocabulary characteristic of the Roman rite should be kept; and that the anthropomorphisms, metaphors, and images in the original text should be preserved. In this second part, we are also given some rules about the adaptations that can be made upon translating to the vernacular language, and norms are given about the auditory and oral dimensions of the translations. A third of this document occupies itself with the questions on syntax, style, person, number and genre, and finally offers the rules of translation of the terms in Greek and Hebrew.

Finally, *Ratio Translationis* complements *Liturgiam Authenticam* insofar as it refers to details for the translation of the liturgical texts from Latin (or *editio tipica)* into English.

CONCLUSION

It is projected that the third edition of the *Roman Missal* in English will be ready for sale by publishing houses in 2011, prior to the beginning of Advent. By Advent of 2011, the use of the new *Missal* in English will begin in the celebrations of the holy Eucharist.

Meanwhile, what will happen to the Masses celebrated in Spanish in the United States? The Committee of Divine Worship in the Episcopal Conference in the United States has a subcommittee that is working on the preparation of the third edition of the *Roman Missal* in Spanish. This subcommittee has not finished this edition. Once this group finishes the *Roman Missal* text in Spanish, it will be ready to be presented to the United States Conference of Catholic Bishops (USCCB) for their approval. If the bishops approve the text, it will be sent to Rome to the Congregation for Divine Worship and the Discipline of the Sacraments for their final approval, known as a *recognitio*. While this process of preparation of the third edition for the Spanish *Missal* is under way, the current *Missal* will continue to be used.

As was seen in this book, in its short history, the liturgy continues to be a living liturgy and will continue evolving. As Archbishop Piero Marini said on the occasion of the publication of his book, *A Challenging Reform*, "the future of the liturgy is the future of the Church."[19] His observation is very accurate since it is in the liturgy that the Church finds its identity. It is in the liturgy that the Church finds its ecclesiastical community, the mystical body of Christ. In the liturgy, the Church also finds its end and feeds itself as from a spring. Whether it is in English or in Spanish, we will soon have a new text for the liturgy of the Mass. It is very important that we have the means of communication to inform and train the people of God to receive the new translation of the third edition of the *Roman Missal*. In this way, we can be ready to respond to the call of the Constitution on the Sacred Liturgy, *Sacrosanctum Concilium*, to facilitate the full, conscious, and active participation of the faithful in the liturgy.

---

19 *The Genius of the Roman Rite*, p. 115